For my little birds...
Matthew, Emma, & Joshua

I Love You, Little Bird

By Jennaya Joy Monroe
Illustrated by Elyse Whittaker-Paek

Printed in Korea by asianprinting.com
Library of Congress Control Number: 2012915857
ISBN 978-0-615-67257-1

A mother bird and
baby bird sat on a
branch and began to talk.

"Mommy," said the baby bird,
"I know that you love me, but will
you always love me?"

"I will *always* love you," said the mommy bird.

The baby bird thought for a moment.

"Mommy, I know that you love me," he said, "but what if I roll in the dirt and get mud all over my face and feathers?"

"If you roll in the dirt," said the mommy bird, "and get mud all over your face and feathers, then together we will wash you clean and I will still love you."

The little bird liked his mother's response.

Then he asked, "Mommy, I know that you love me, but what if I go on a great adventure and fly too far away?"

"If you go on a great adventure and fly too far away," said the mommy bird, "then I will chase after you as fast as I can. I will not give up until I catch you and bring you home to me."

"And I will still love you."

The baby bird was pleased with his mother's reply, but had another question to ask.

"Mommy, I know that you love me, but what if I bump our nest and it falls to the ground and breaks into a thousand pieces?"

"If you bump our nest and it falls to the ground..."

"...and breaks into a thousand pieces," said the mommy bird, "then together we will rebuild our nest and make it stronger and more beautiful than before; and I will still love you."

The little bird was happy with his mommy's answers.

Then one day as the little bird was playing in the flowers he heard the sound of many wings flapping. When he looked up...

...he saw his flock was flying away. He started toward the birds, but his leg became tangled in a vine.

He saw his mother from a distance
and cried out, "Mommy, wait
for me! Don't leave!"

The mother bird left the flock and untangled the little bird. She pulled her baby close and said, "Let all the rest fly away. I will stay behind with you. You are my little bird, and I will *always* love you."

"Good," said the little bird.
And he snuggled under his mother's
wing and fell asleep.

"...He gently leads those that have young." Isaiah 40:11